PROJECT
2025

The Citizen's Guide to America's Next Political Era

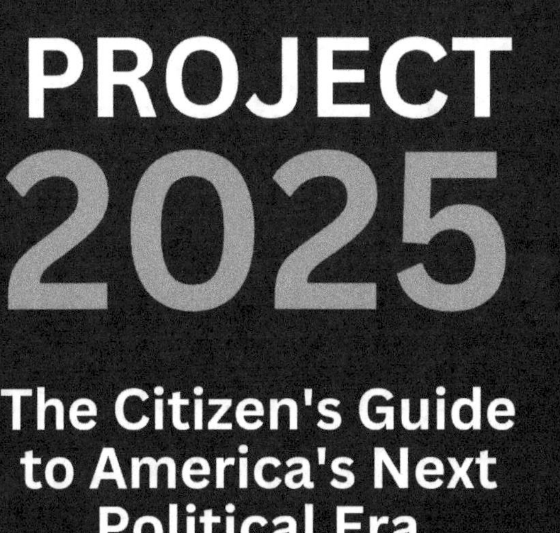

B W. Dorman

Project 2025

The Citizen's Guide to America's Next Political Era

B W. Dorman

Copyright

Disclaimer

The information contained in this book is for general informational purposes only. The author has made every effort to ensure the accuracy of the information provided; however, the author assumes no responsibility for errors or omissions, or for damages resulting from the use of the information contained herein. The opinions expressed in this book are those of the author and do not necessarily reflect the views of any organizations or institutions with which the author is affiliated.

Introduction

A Personal Journey into America's Political Future

Dear Reader,

As I sit down to write this introduction, I am reminded of the countless conversations I've had with friends, family, and strangers alike about the future of our great nation. Like many of you, I have felt a mix of hope, anxiety, and curiosity about what lies ahead.

It was during one particularly engaging discussion with my grandfather—a man who has lived through some of the most transformative periods in American history—that the seed for this book was planted.

Grandpa's stories of resilience during the Great Depression, his unwavering spirit through the civil rights movement, and his pride in voting during pivotal elections have always inspired me.

It was his belief in the power of informed citizenship that led me to create "Project 2025: The Citizen's Guide to America's Next Political Era." This book is my heartfelt attempt to bring clarity, understanding, and empowerment to every reader who, like me, seeks to navigate the complexities of our political landscape with confidence.

Join me as we explore the nuances of Project 2025, a critical juncture in our nation's history. Together, we will delve into the challenges and opportunities that lie ahead, armed with knowledge and a shared sense of purpose. Let's embark on this journey together, as friends and fellow citizens, eager to understand and shape the future of America.

Chapter 1: The Genesis of Project 2025

Introduction to Project 2025: What It Is and Why It Matters

Project 2025 is not just another policy initiative; it is a comprehensive blueprint designed to reshape the political, economic, and social landscape of the United States. The essence of Project 2025 lies in its ambition to address the critical issues facing our nation and to pave the way for a more resilient and prosperous future.

This initiative encompasses a wide range of policies, from healthcare reform and economic revitalization to educational advancements and environmental sustainability.

The significance of Project 2025 cannot be overstated. As we approach a pivotal moment in our nation's history, the decisions made under this initiative will have far-reaching implications for generations to come.

Understanding Project 2025 is crucial for every citizen who wishes to engage meaningfully in the democratic process and contribute to shaping the future of America.

Historical Context: Key Events Leading Up to This Initiative

To fully appreciate the genesis of Project 2025, it is essential to understand the historical context that has shaped its development. Over the past few decades, the United States has experienced a series of transformative events that have highlighted both the strengths and vulnerabilities of our nation.

1. The Great Recession (2008-2009): This economic crisis exposed significant weaknesses in the financial system, leading to widespread unemployment and a dramatic increase in public debt. The aftermath of the recession sparked debates about regulatory reforms and the role of government in stabilizing the economy.

2. The Affordable Care Act (2010): Also known as Obamacare, this landmark legislation aimed to expand healthcare coverage and reduce costs. While it achieved significant milestones, it also faced substantial opposition and legal challenges, underscoring the complexities of healthcare reform.

3. The Rise of Social Movements (2010s): Movements such as Black Lives Matter and MeToo brought issues of racial justice, gender equality, and police reform to the forefront of national discourse. These movements highlighted the need for systemic change and greater inclusivity in American society.

4. The COVID-19 Pandemic (2020): The global pandemic revealed profound gaps in the nation's public health infrastructure and exacerbated economic inequalities. The response to COVID-19 underscored the importance of robust healthcare systems, economic support measures, and effective governance.

5. Political Polarization and the 2020 Election: The contentious 2020 presidential election and subsequent events, including the Capitol riot on January 6, 2021, highlighted deep divisions within the country. These events underscored the need for efforts to bridge political divides and restore faith in democratic institutions.

My First Encounter with the Concept of Project 2025

I vividly remember the first time I heard about Project 2025. It was during a family gathering in the summer of 2023. My uncle, a passionate advocate for political reform, brought up the topic over dinner. As he spoke about the ambitious goals of Project 2025, I felt a mix of intrigue and skepticism. Could such a comprehensive plan truly address the myriad challenges facing our nation?

My uncle, ever the optimist, shared his vision of a future where every American had access to quality healthcare, where the economy thrived on sustainable practices, and where education was a right, not a privilege. His enthusiasm was infectious, and I found myself wanting to learn more.

In the weeks that followed, I delved into research, reading policy papers, attending webinars, and engaging in discussions with experts and advocates.
The more I learned, the more I realized the transformative potential of Project 2025.

It became clear that this initiative was not just a collection of policies but a cohesive strategy aimed at creating a better future for all Americans.

The Vision Behind Project 2025

At its core, Project 2025 is driven by a vision of a more equitable, sustainable, and prosperous America. The architects of this initiative have laid out a roadmap that addresses key areas of concern:

1. Economic Revitalization: Emphasizing job creation, wage growth, and support for small businesses, Project 2025 aims to build a resilient economy that works for everyone. This includes investments in infrastructure, green energy, and technological innovation.

2. Healthcare Reform: Recognizing the critical importance of healthcare, Project 2025 proposes a series of reforms to expand coverage, reduce costs, and improve the quality of care.
This includes strengthening public health systems and ensuring access to essential services for all citizens.

3. Educational Advancements: Education is the cornerstone of a thriving society. Project 2025 advocates for comprehensive educational reforms, including increased funding for public schools, affordable higher education, and vocational training programs to prepare the workforce for the jobs of the future.

4. Environmental Sustainability: Addressing climate change and promoting environmental stewardship are central to Project 2025. The initiative includes policies aimed at reducing carbon emissions, protecting natural resources, and fostering sustainable practices across industries.

5. Social Justice and Inclusivity: Project 2025 is committed to advancing social justice and ensuring that all Americans, regardless of race, gender, or socioeconomic status, have equal opportunities. This includes criminal justice reform, anti-discrimination measures, and initiatives to promote diversity and inclusion.

As we embark on this exploration of Project 2025, it is important to remember that this initiative is not just about policies and reforms; it is about the people whose lives will be impacted by these changes.
It is about the hopes and dreams of millions of Americans who aspire to a better future for themselves and their families.

In the chapters that follow, we will delve deeper into the specific components of Project 2025, examining the challenges and opportunities that lie ahead. Together, we will gain a comprehensive understanding of this transformative initiative and explore how each of us can play a role in shaping the future of our nation.

Chapter 2: The Political Landscape Today

Current State of Affairs: An Overview of the Political Environment in 2024

As we delve into the present political landscape of 2024, it is clear that the United States stands at a crossroads. The country is grappling with a myriad of challenges, from economic instability and healthcare crises to deep-seated social inequalities and environmental concerns. These issues are compounded by a highly polarized political climate that has made consensus-building increasingly difficult.

The political environment today is characterized by sharp divisions along party lines, with Republicans and Democrats often finding themselves at odds over key policy issues.

The aftermath of the 2020 election, followed by the tumultuous events of January 6, 2021, has left an indelible mark on the nation's psyche. Trust in governmental institutions is at a historic low, and many Americans feel disillusioned with the political process.

Amidst this backdrop, the 2024 election cycle has brought new voices and perspectives to the forefront. Emerging political movements and third-party candidates are challenging the traditional two-party system, advocating for a more inclusive and representative democracy. This evolving landscape presents both opportunities and challenges as the nation seeks to navigate a path forward.

Key Political Figures and Their Roles

To understand the current political climate, it is essential to familiarize ourselves with the major players shaping the discourse and driving policy decisions. These key political figures wield significant influence over the direction of the country and play crucial roles in shaping the future of American politics.

1. The President: The sitting president remains a central figure in the political landscape, with the power to set the national agenda and influence legislative priorities.
Their policies and actions are closely scrutinized and often serve as a barometer for the nation's political health.

2. Congressional Leaders: The leaders of the Senate and the House of Representatives hold considerable sway over the legislative process. Their ability to negotiate, build coalitions, and navigate partisan divides is critical to the passage of key legislation.

3. State Governors: Governors play a pivotal role in shaping state-level policies and implementing federal directives. Their actions can have far-reaching implications for the national political landscape, particularly in areas such as healthcare, education, and economic development.

4. Political Activists and Advocates: Grassroots movements and advocacy groups have become increasingly influential in shaping public opinion and driving policy changes. Figures such as community organizers, social justice advocates, and environmental activists are mobilizing citizens and pushing for systemic reforms.

5. Media Personalities: In an age of information saturation, media figures and pundits hold significant power in framing political narratives and influencing public perception. Their commentary can shape the national discourse and impact the political fortunes of candidates and parties.

Reflecting on the Political Changes I Have Witnessed

Reflecting on the political changes I have witnessed over the past few decades, I am struck by the rapid pace of transformation and the profound impact these shifts have had on our society. Growing up, I remember a time when political discourse, while contentious, seemed more rooted in mutual respect and a shared commitment to the common good.

One of my earliest political memories is watching the presidential debates with my parents. The candidates, despite their differences, engaged in spirited yet respectful exchanges. It was a time when bipartisanship seemed possible, and there was a sense of optimism about the future of our democracy.

However, as I entered adulthood, I began to notice a shift. The rise of social media and 24-hour news cycles brought new challenges, as political discourse became increasingly polarized and sensationalized.

The lines between fact and opinion began to blur, and trust in traditional media sources waned.

The 2020 election was a turning point for me. The contentious nature of the campaign, coupled with the unprecedented events of the Capitol riot, left me feeling disheartened and uncertain about the future of our nation. It was during this time that I realized the importance of staying informed and actively engaged in the political process.

My journey to understand Project 2025 has been both enlightening and empowering. It has reinforced my belief that informed citizenship is the cornerstone of a healthy democracy. By gaining a deeper understanding of the political landscape and the key players involved, we can better navigate the complexities of our current environment and work towards meaningful change.

The Role of Technology in Modern Politics

Technology has revolutionized the way we engage with politics, offering both opportunities and challenges. Social media platforms, in particular, have transformed political communication, enabling politicians to connect directly with constituents and mobilize supporters. However, these platforms have also facilitated the spread of misinformation and contributed to the polarization of political discourse.

1. Social Media: Platforms like Twitter, Facebook, and Instagram have become essential tools for political campaigns, allowing candidates to reach vast audiences and engage with voters in real-time. However, the rapid dissemination of information can also amplify false narratives and deepen political divides.

2. Data Analytics: The use of data analytics in political campaigns has increased dramatically, allowing candidates to target specific demographics and tailor their messaging. While this can enhance voter engagement, it also raises concerns about privacy and the manipulation of public opinion.

3. Digital Activism: Technology has empowered grassroots movements and advocacy groups, enabling them to organize, mobilize, and effect change on a scale previously unimaginable. Digital activism has played a crucial role in raising awareness and driving policy changes on issues such as climate change, social justice, and healthcare reform.

The political landscape of 2024 is a complex and dynamic environment, shaped by a myriad of factors and key players. Understanding this landscape is essential for navigating the challenges and opportunities that lie ahead. By staying informed and engaged, we can contribute to shaping a future that reflects our shared values and aspirations.

As we continue our exploration of Project 2025, it is important to keep in mind the broader context in which this initiative operates.

The challenges we face are significant, but so too are the opportunities for positive change.Together, we can work towards a more inclusive, equitable, and sustainable future for all Americans.

Chapter 3: Understanding Governance Shifts

Key Changes: Analyzing the Major Shifts in Governance Proposed by Project 2025

Project 2025 is set to introduce several transformative changes in the way our government operates. These shifts are designed to address systemic issues and modernize the infrastructure of governance to better meet the needs of a 21st-century society. To fully grasp the impact of these changes, it is essential to break down the key areas of reform proposed by this ambitious initiative.

1. Decentralization of Power: One of the cornerstone policies of Project 2025 is the decentralization of federal power, aiming to give more autonomy to state and local governments. This shift is intended to foster innovation and tailored solutions that are more closely aligned with the unique needs of diverse communities across the nation.

2. Enhanced Transparency and Accountability: The initiative emphasizes the need for greater transparency and accountability within government institutions. This includes implementing rigorous oversight mechanisms, enhancing whistleblower protections, and increasing public access to governmental data. These measures are designed to rebuild trust in government and ensure that officials are held accountable for their actions.

3. Digital Transformation: Recognizing the growing importance of technology, Project 2025 proposes a comprehensive digital transformation of governmental operations. This involves modernizing IT infrastructure, adopting advanced data analytics, and implementing secure digital platforms for public services. The goal is to improve efficiency, accessibility, and responsiveness in government interactions.

4. Citizen Engagement: Engaging citizens in the democratic process is a central theme of Project 2025. The initiative seeks to create more opportunities for public participation, from town hall meetings and online forums to participatory budgeting and civic education programs.

These efforts aim to empower citizens and foster a more inclusive and participatory democracy.

5. Sustainable Governance: Addressing environmental challenges is a key priority for Project 2025. The initiative includes policies to integrate sustainability into all aspects of governance, from reducing carbon emissions and promoting renewable energy to implementing green building standards and encouraging sustainable agriculture.

Implications for Citizens: How These Changes Will Affect Everyday Americans

The proposed shifts in governance are poised to have a significant impact on the lives of everyday Americans. Understanding these implications can help citizens prepare for and adapt to the changes that lie ahead.

1. Greater Local Influence: By decentralizing power, Project 2025 aims to give communities more control over their own destinies. This means that citizens will have a greater say in local decision-making processes, potentially leading to policies that are more closely aligned with their specific needs and preferences.

2. Improved Government Services: The digital transformation of government operations is expected to streamline processes and enhance the quality of public services. Citizens can look forward to more efficient and user-friendly interactions with government agencies, from applying for permits and licenses to accessing social services and benefits.

3. Increased Accountability: Enhanced transparency and accountability measures are designed to ensure that government officials act in the best interests of the public. Citizens can expect greater oversight of governmental actions and more robust mechanisms for holding officials accountable for misconduct or negligence.

4. Enhanced Civic Participation: Project 2025's focus on citizen engagement aims to create a more vibrant and inclusive democracy. Citizens will have more opportunities to participate in the political process, influence policy decisions, and collaborate on community projects. This increased involvement can lead to a stronger sense of civic responsibility and empowerment.

5. Sustainable Living: The emphasis on sustainable governance will promote environmentally-friendly practices across various sectors. Citizens can anticipate more green spaces, cleaner air and water, and increased access to renewable energy sources. These changes are expected to enhance the overall quality of life and contribute to a healthier planet for future generations.

Expert Opinions: Insights from Political Analysts and Scholars

To gain a deeper understanding of the implications of Project 2025, it is valuable to consider the perspectives of political analysts and scholars who have studied the initiative extensively. Their insights can provide a nuanced view of the potential benefits and challenges associated with the proposed governance shifts.

1. Decentralization and Innovation: According to Dr. Emily T. decentralizing power can lead to greater innovation at the local level. "When local governments have the autonomy to experiment with new policies and approaches, they can develop more effective solutions tailored to their specific contexts," she explains. However, Dr. Emily also cautions that this approach requires robust mechanisms for sharing best practices and ensuring equity across regions.

2. Digital Transformation and Efficiency: James Stevens, a technology policy expert, highlights the potential of digital transformation to revolutionize government operations. "By leveraging advanced technologies, governments can become more agile, efficient, and responsive to the needs of citizens," he notes. Stevens emphasizes the importance of cybersecurity measures to protect sensitive data and maintain public trust in digital platforms.

3. Citizen Engagement and Democracy: Political analyst S. Martinez underscores the significance of enhanced civic participation in strengthening democracy. "Engaging citizens in the political process not only empowers individuals but also fosters a more inclusive and representative governance," she asserts. Martinez advocates for comprehensive civic education programs to equip citizens with the knowledge and skills needed to participate effectively.

4. Sustainable Governance and Environmental Protection: Environmental policy scholar Dr. Michael Reed praises Project 2025's commitment to sustainability. "Integrating sustainability into governance is essential for addressing the urgent challenges of climate change and environmental degradation," he states. Dr. Reed emphasizes the need for collaboration between government, industry, and civil society to achieve meaningful progress.

The governance shifts proposed by Project 2025 represent a bold and forward-thinking approach to addressing the complex challenges facing our nation. By decentralizing power, enhancing transparency, embracing digital transformation, fostering citizen engagement, and promoting sustainability, this initiative aims to create a more responsive, inclusive, and resilient government.

As we continue our exploration of Project 2025, it is important to remain informed and engaged. The changes outlined in this chapter have the potential to transform our political landscape and improve the lives of citizens across the country. By understanding these shifts and their implications, we can better navigate the evolving governance environment and contribute to shaping a brighter future for all Americans.

Chapter 4: The Role of Media in Shaping Public Perception

Media Influence: Examining the Media's Role in Politics

The media has always played a critical role in shaping public perception and influencing political outcomes. In today's digital age, its impact is more profound than ever. From traditional newspapers and television broadcasts to social media platforms and online news outlets, the media serves as the primary conduit through which citizens receive information about political events, policies, and figures.

The role of the media in politics can be seen through several key functions:

1. Information Dissemination: The media provides the public with essential information about political developments, government actions, and societal issues. It helps keep citizens informed and aware of what is happening at local, national, and international levels.

2. Agenda-Setting: By selecting which issues to highlight, the media can influence the public agenda. The topics that receive the most coverage often become the most salient issues for voters and policymakers alike.

3. Framing: The way in which news stories are presented can significantly affect public perception. Through framing, the media can shape how people interpret and understand political events and issues.

4. Watchdog Function: The media acts as a watchdog, holding government officials and institutions accountable. Investigative journalism can uncover corruption, abuse of power, and other misconduct, prompting public scrutiny and legal action.

5. Public Opinion Shaping: Through editorials, opinion pieces, and pundit commentary, the media helps shape public opinion. Influential media personalities and outlets can sway public attitudes and perceptions on various political matters.

Instances of Media Impact on Political Outcomes

To illustrate the media's influence on political outcomes, let's examine several notable case studies where media coverage played a pivotal role.

1. The Watergate Scandal (1972-1974): The investigative journalism of The Washington Post, led by reporters Bob Woodward and Carl Bernstein, uncovered the Watergate scandal, leading to the resignation of President Richard Nixon. The media's relentless pursuit of the truth demonstrated its power to hold the highest office in the land accountable.

2. The 2008 Presidential Election: The rise of social media platforms like Facebook and Twitter transformed political campaigning.
Barack Obama's campaign effectively leveraged these platforms to mobilize young voters, disseminate campaign messages, and counter misinformation. The media's role in this election underscored the growing importance of digital engagement.

3. The Arab Spring (2010-2011): Social media played a crucial role in the Arab Spring uprisings across the Middle East and North Africa. Platforms like Twitter and Facebook were used to organize protests, share information, and document government crackdowns. The media's influence in these movements highlighted its ability to facilitate political change.

4. The 2016 Presidential Election: The 2016 election saw the proliferation of "fake news" and misinformation on social media, significantly impacting public perception and voter behavior. The media's role in both disseminating and combating misinformation became a central issue, raising questions about media responsibility and credibility.

How Media Has Shaped My Own Political Views

Reflecting on my own experiences, I can attest to the profound impact that the media has had on shaping my political views. Growing up, my family was avid consumers of news, with the evening newscast being a staple in our household. I vividly remember watching coverage of major events like the fall of the Berlin Wall and the 9/11 attacks, events that left an indelible mark on my understanding of the world.

As I entered adulthood, my media consumption habits evolved. The rise of digital media and social networks provided me with access to a diverse array of perspectives and information sources. However, this abundance of information also made it challenging to discern fact from fiction. I learned the importance of critical thinking and media literacy, skills that have become essential in navigating today's complex media landscape.

One particular instance that stands out is the 2016 election. The media coverage was intense, and the constant barrage of conflicting information left me feeling overwhelmed and uncertain. It was during this time that I realized the need to seek out reliable sources, cross-check information, and engage in thoughtful discussions with others. This experience reinforced my belief in the power of an informed and engaged citizenry.

The Evolution of Media: From Traditional to Digital

The media landscape has undergone a dramatic transformation over the past few decades. Traditional media, such as newspapers, television, and radio, once dominated the dissemination of news and information. However, the advent of the internet and digital technologies has revolutionized the way we consume media.

1. The Rise of Online News: Digital news outlets and blogs have proliferated, offering real-time updates and a wide range of perspectives. This shift has democratized access to information but has also led to challenges related to misinformation and the credibility of sources.

2. Social Media Platforms: Platforms like Facebook, Twitter, Instagram, and YouTube have become central to the way people share and consume news. These platforms enable rapid dissemination of information but also facilitate the spread of misinformation and echo chambers.

3. Citizen Journalism: The digital age has given rise to citizen journalism, where ordinary individuals use smartphones and social media to report on events. While this has expanded the range of voices in the media landscape, it also raises questions about accuracy and journalistic standards.

4. The Decline of Print Media: Traditional print media has faced significant challenges, with many newspapers and magazines experiencing declining circulation and revenue. This has led to layoffs, mergers, and the closure of some long-standing publications.

Challenges and Opportunities in the Digital Age

The digital age presents both challenges and opportunities for the media and its role in shaping public perception.

1. Misinformation and Fake News: The spread of false information poses a significant threat to informed citizenship. Combating misinformation requires robust fact-checking, media literacy education, and responsible platform management.

2. Echo Chambers and Polarization: Social media algorithms often create echo chambers, where users are exposed primarily to information that reinforces their existing beliefs. This can deepen political polarization and hinder constructive dialogue.

3. Opportunities for Engagement: Digital platforms offer unprecedented opportunities for citizen engagement and participation. From online petitions to virtual town halls, technology can facilitate greater involvement in the democratic process.

4. The Role of Algorithms: Algorithms that prioritize sensational or divisive content can distort public perception and discourse. There is a growing need for transparency and ethical considerations in algorithm design and implementation.

The media's role in shaping public perception and influencing political outcomes is undeniable. As we navigate the complexities of the digital age, it is crucial to remain vigilant, critical, and engaged consumers of media. By understanding the media's influence and the challenges it faces, we can better navigate the information landscape and contribute to a more informed and vibrant democracy.

As we continue our exploration of Project 2025, let us remember the power of the media to inform, influence, and inspire. By fostering media literacy and encouraging responsible journalism, we can ensure that the media serves as a force for good in our society.

Chapter 5: The Power of Civic Engagement

Importance of Participation: Why Every Vote and Voice Matters

Civic engagement is the lifeblood of a thriving democracy. It encompasses the ways in which citizens participate in the political process, from voting and attending town hall meetings to volunteering and engaging in community activism. The importance of civic engagement cannot be overstated; it is the foundation upon which a responsive and accountable government is built.

Every vote and every voice matters. When citizens actively participate in the political process, they help shape the policies and decisions that affect their daily lives. Civic engagement ensures that diverse perspectives are represented and that elected officials are held accountable to the people they serve.
It fosters a sense of ownership and responsibility, empowering individuals to contribute to the common good.

Moreover, civic engagement is a powerful antidote to political apathy and disenfranchisement. In an era where trust in institutions is waning, active participation can restore faith in the democratic process. It reminds us that democracy is not a spectator sport; it requires the active involvement of all citizens to function effectively.

How to Get Involved: Practical Ways to Engage in the Political Process

Engaging in the political process can take many forms, from traditional methods like voting to more hands-on approaches like community organizing. Here are some practical ways to get involved:

1. Voting: Voting is the most direct way to influence government and policy. Make sure you are registered to vote and participate in local, state, and national elections. Encourage friends and family to do the same.

2. Contacting Elected Officials: Reach out to your elected representatives to express your views on important issues. Writing letters, making phone calls, and sending emails are effective ways to communicate your concerns and advocate for change.

3. Attending Town Hall Meetings: Town hall meetings provide an opportunity to engage directly with elected officials and participate in discussions about community issues. Attend these meetings to ask questions, provide input, and stay informed about local developments.

4. Joining Advocacy Groups: Advocacy groups and non-profit organizations work on a wide range of issues, from environmental protection to social justice. Joining these groups allows you to collaborate with others who share your interests and work towards common goals.

5. Volunteering: Volunteering for political campaigns, community organizations, and local events is a hands-on way to make a difference. It provides valuable experience and helps build networks of like-minded individuals.

6. Participating in Protests and Rallies: Peaceful protests and rallies are powerful tools for raising awareness and advocating for change. Participate in events that align with your values to show solidarity and amplify your voice.

7. Engaging on Social Media: Use social media platforms to share information, raise awareness, and mobilize support for causes you care about. Engage in respectful and constructive dialogue to promote understanding and action.

8. Civic Education: Educate yourself and others about the political process, key issues, and ways to get involved. Host discussion groups, workshops, and educational events to foster civic literacy in your community.

Inspiring Stories: Profiles of Ordinary Citizens Making a Difference

The impact of civic engagement is best illustrated through the inspiring stories of ordinary citizens who have made a difference in their communities and beyond.

These individuals demonstrate that anyone, regardless of background or resources, can contribute to positive change.

1. Stacey Abrams: Stacey Abrams' work in voter registration and advocacy has transformed the political landscape in Georgia. Her efforts to combat voter suppression and mobilize underrepresented communities played a crucial role in the state's recent electoral outcomes.

2. Greta Thunberg: As a young climate activist, Greta Thunberg has inspired a global movement to address climate change. Her passionate advocacy and grassroots organizing have brought attention to environmental issues and mobilized millions of people worldwide.

3. Malala Yousafzai: Malala Yousafzai's courageous advocacy for girls' education in Pakistan has had a profound impact on global education policies. Despite facing significant danger, she has continued to champion the right to education for all children.

4. Tarana Burke: The founder of the MeToo movement, Tarana Burke, has brought attention to issues of sexual violence and harassment. Her work has empowered survivors to speak out and has sparked important conversations about consent and accountability.

5. José Andrés: Renowned chef José Andrés has used his platform to provide disaster relief and support communities in crisis through his organization, World Central Kitchen. His efforts to feed those in need during natural disasters and the COVID-19 pandemic exemplify the power of civic engagement.

The Impact of Grassroots Movements

Grassroots movements are a testament to the power of collective action. These movements are often driven by passionate individuals who come together to address specific issues and advocate for change from the ground up. Their decentralized and community-focused approach can lead to significant and lasting impacts.

1. Black Lives Matter: The Black Lives Matter movement, founded in 2013, has brought global attention to issues of racial injustice and police brutality. Through protests, advocacy, and community organizing, the movement has sparked widespread dialogue and policy changes aimed at addressing systemic racism.

2. March for Our Lives: In response to the tragic school shooting in Parkland, Florida, students organized the March for Our Lives movement to advocate for gun control and safer schools.
Their activism has led to increased awareness and legislative efforts to address gun violence.

3. Women's March: The Women's March, which began in 2017, mobilized millions of people worldwide to advocate for women's rights and social justice. The movement has continued to push for gender equality, reproductive rights, and other critical issues.

4. Sunrise Movement: The Sunrise Movement is a youth-led organization focused on combating climate change and advocating for a Green New Deal.

Their grassroots efforts have brought climate issues to the forefront of political discourse and inspired a new generation of environmental activists.

Civic engagement is a powerful force for change. By participating in the political process and advocating for issues we care about, we can shape the future of our communities and our nation. The inspiring stories of individuals and grassroots movements remind us that every action, no matter how small, can make a difference.

As we continue our exploration of Project 2025, let us remain committed to the principles of active citizenship and collective action. Together, we can build a more just, equitable, and democratic society.

Chapter 6: Navigating Political Polarization

Understanding Polarization: Causes and Consequences of Political Division

Political polarization has become a defining feature of contemporary American politics. It refers to the growing ideological divide between political parties, which manifests in increasingly partisan attitudes and behaviors among both politicians and the public. This polarization is not just a difference in opinion but a deep-seated division that affects the way people perceive and interact with those who hold opposing views.

Several factors contribute to this polarization:

1. Media Environment: The rise of 24-hour news cycles and the proliferation of partisan media outlets have created echo chambers where individuals are exposed primarily to information that reinforces their existing beliefs. This media environment exacerbates divisions by promoting sensationalized and polarized content.

2. Social Media: Social media platforms amplify polarization by facilitating the rapid spread of information and enabling users to curate their information bubbles. Algorithms often prioritize content that generates strong emotional reactions, further deepening ideological divides.

3. Political Strategy: Politicians and parties often exploit polarization for strategic gain. By mobilizing their base with divisive rhetoric, they can energize supporters and suppress turnout among opponents. This strategy can lead to a more polarized electorate and legislative gridlock.

4. Economic Inequality: Growing economic inequality has fueled resentment and mistrust among different socioeconomic groups. Disparities in wealth and opportunity contribute to a sense of injustice and alienation, which can be exploited by populist movements and leaders.

5. Cultural Shifts: Cultural changes, such as shifts in demographics and social norms, have also played a role in increasing polarization. Issues related to race, gender, and immigration often serve as flashpoints for ideological conflict.

The consequences of political polarization are profound and far-reaching:

1. Legislative Gridlock: Polarization often leads to legislative gridlock, where parties are unable or unwilling to compromise on key issues. This can result in policy paralysis and hinder the government's ability to address pressing challenges.

2. Erosion of Trust: Polarization erodes trust in political institutions and democratic processes. When individuals perceive that their views are not represented or that the system is rigged against them, their faith in democracy diminishes.

3. Social Fragmentation: The ideological divide extends beyond politics, affecting social relationships and communities. Polarization can lead to increased social fragmentation, where individuals become isolated within their ideological groups and distrustful of others.

4. Threats to Democracy: Extreme polarization can undermine the stability of democratic institutions. When political divisions become so entrenched that compromise and cooperation are impossible, the risk of democratic backsliding increases.

Bridging the Gap: Strategies for Fostering Dialogue and Understanding

Addressing political polarization requires concerted efforts to bridge the gap between opposing sides and foster a more inclusive and constructive dialogue. Here are some strategies to consider:

1. Promoting Media Literacy: Educating citizens about media literacy can help them critically evaluate the information they consume and recognize bias and misinformation. This can reduce the impact of partisan media and encourage more balanced perspectives.

2. Encouraging Cross-Ideological Dialogue: Creating opportunities for individuals to engage in dialogue with those who hold different views can help break down stereotypes and build mutual understanding. Programs that facilitate respectful and open conversations can bridge ideological divides.

3. Fostering Civic Education: Civic education programs that emphasize the principles of democracy, the importance of compromise, and the value of diverse perspectives can equip citizens with the knowledge and skills needed to navigate a polarized political landscape.

4. Supporting Bipartisan Initiatives: Encouraging bipartisan initiatives and collaborations can demonstrate that cooperation is possible even in a polarized environment. Highlighting successful examples of cross-party cooperation can inspire others to seek common ground.

5. Addressing Economic Inequality: Tackling the root causes of economic inequality can reduce the resentment and mistrust that fuel polarization. Policies that promote economic opportunity and social mobility can help create a more equitable and cohesive society.

6. Reforming Political Practices: Reforms aimed at reducing the influence of money in politics, promoting fair electoral processes, and encouraging greater representation can help mitigate the strategic incentives for polarization.

My Journey Towards Finding Common Ground

Reflecting on my own journey, I realize that navigating political polarization has been a challenging but rewarding process. Like many others, I have experienced moments of frustration and disillusionment, feeling that meaningful dialogue was impossible in such a divided environment.

One pivotal experience occurred during a community forum on healthcare reform. The room was filled with individuals from various political backgrounds, each passionately advocating for their perspectives. Initially, the discussions were heated, and it seemed that consensus was out of reach.

However, as the evening progressed, something remarkable happened. Participants began to listen—truly listen—to each other's stories and concerns. I shared my own experiences with the healthcare system, and others did the same. We discovered that despite our ideological differences, we shared common goals: access to affordable care, quality treatment, and support for vulnerable populations.

This experience taught me the power of empathy and understanding. By focusing on our shared humanity rather than our differences, we were able to find common ground and develop practical solutions. It was a reminder that while polarization is a significant challenge, it is not insurmountable.

Initiatives and Programs Promoting Unity

Several initiatives and programs have been successful in promoting unity and bridging ideological divides. These efforts provide valuable lessons and models for fostering dialogue and understanding in a polarized environment.

1. Living Room Conversations: This initiative brings people together for structured conversations on specific topics, encouraging participants to share their personal experiences and perspectives. By fostering respectful dialogue, Living Room Conversations helps build bridges between individuals with differing views.

2. Better Angels: Better Angels is a bipartisan organization dedicated to depolarizing America by facilitating workshops and discussions that encourage understanding and cooperation. Their programs aim to reduce stereotypes and foster empathy among participants.

3. BridgeUSA: BridgeUSA is a student-led organization that promotes constructive political discourse on college campuses. Through debates, discussions, and events, BridgeUSA encourages students to engage with diverse viewpoints and develop critical thinking skills.

4. The National Institute for Civil Discourse (NICD): NICD works to promote civility in public discourse by providing training and resources for elected officials, journalists, and community leaders. Their initiatives aim to foster respectful and productive dialogue in the political arena.

Political polarization is a significant challenge, but it is not insurmountable. By understanding the causes and consequences of polarization and implementing strategies to foster dialogue and understanding, we can bridge the ideological divide and build a more cohesive and resilient society.

As we continue our exploration of Project 2025, let us remain committed to the principles of empathy, respect, and cooperation. Together, we can navigate the complexities of political polarization and work towards a future where diverse perspectives are valued and constructive dialogue prevails.

Chapter 7: The Future of American Democracy

Predictions and Projections: What Experts Foresee for America's Political Future

As we look ahead to the future of American democracy, it is clear that the landscape will be shaped by a combination of ongoing trends, emerging challenges, and new opportunities. Political analysts and scholars have offered a range of predictions and projections, highlighting both potential risks and avenues for positive change.

1. Technological Integration: The integration of technology into the political process is expected to continue, with advancements in digital voting systems, blockchain technology for secure elections, and AI-driven policy analysis. These innovations have the potential to enhance transparency, efficiency, and accessibility in governance.

2. Demographic Shifts: The United States is experiencing significant demographic changes, with increasing diversity in terms of race, ethnicity, and age. These shifts will likely influence voting patterns, policy priorities, and political representation, leading to a more inclusive and representative democracy.

3. Climate Change and Sustainability: Climate change will remain a critical issue, with growing demands for policies that address environmental sustainability. The political future will likely see increased emphasis on green energy, conservation efforts, and international cooperation to combat climate change.

4. Economic Inequality: Addressing economic inequality will be a central challenge. Experts predict that policies aimed at reducing income disparity, improving access to education and healthcare, and promoting economic mobility will be crucial for ensuring social stability and cohesion.

5. Political Polarization: While polarization is expected to persist, there is hope that efforts to bridge divides and foster dialogue will gain momentum. Initiatives promoting civic education, media literacy, and bipartisan cooperation may help mitigate the effects of polarization.

6. Global Influence: America's role on the global stage will continue to evolve. The future will likely see a balance between maintaining traditional alliances and navigating new geopolitical realities. Foreign policy will focus on issues such as cybersecurity, trade, and international cooperation on global challenges.

Opportunities for Change: How Citizens Can Influence Positive Outcomes

The future of American democracy is not predetermined; it is shaped by the actions and choices of its citizens. There are several opportunities for individuals to influence positive outcomes and contribute to a more robust and responsive political system.

1. Engaging in Local Politics: Local government plays a critical role in addressing community needs and implementing policies. By participating in local elections, attending city council meetings, and engaging with local officials, citizens can have a direct impact on their communities.

2. Advocating for Electoral Reform: Efforts to reform the electoral process, such as advocating for ranked-choice voting, combating gerrymandering, and promoting campaign finance transparency, can enhance the fairness and inclusivity of elections.

3. Supporting Civic Education: Civic education is essential for fostering informed and engaged citizens. Supporting programs that teach the principles of democracy, critical thinking, and media literacy can help build a more knowledgeable and active electorate.

4. Promoting Inclusivity: Advocating for policies that promote inclusivity and diversity in political representation can ensure that all voices are heard. This includes supporting candidates from underrepresented groups and championing initiatives that address systemic inequalities.

5. Engaging in Constructive Dialogue: Encouraging respectful and constructive dialogue across ideological lines can help bridge divides and build understanding. Participating in community discussions, joining bipartisan organizations, and practicing active listening are ways to contribute to a healthier political climate.

6. Volunteering and Activism: Volunteering for political campaigns, advocacy groups, and community organizations allows citizens to contribute to causes they care about. Grassroots activism can drive change from the ground up and amplify the voices of ordinary people.

Reflecting on the Journey and Looking Ahead with Hope

As we conclude our exploration of Project 2025 and the future of American democracy, it is important to reflect on the journey we have taken together. Throughout this book, we have examined the key components of Project 2025, delved into the current political landscape, and explored strategies for fostering a more inclusive and resilient democracy.

The future of American democracy is filled with both challenges and opportunities. It will require the collective efforts of informed and engaged citizens to navigate the complexities of the political landscape and shape a future that reflects our shared values and aspirations.

I am reminded of the words of President John F. Kennedy, who once said, "Ask not what your country can do for you—ask what you can do for your country." This call to action resonates deeply as we consider our role in shaping the future of our nation. Each of us has the power to make a difference, to advocate for change, and to contribute to the common good.

As we look ahead, let us do so with hope and determination. Let us embrace the principles of empathy, respect, and cooperation, and work towards a future where every voice is heard, every vote counts, and every individual has the opportunity to thrive.

Thank you for joining me on this journey. Your engagement and commitment to understanding and improving our democracy are truly inspiring. Together, we can build a brighter, more inclusive, and more democratic future for all.

Conclusion: A Call to Action

Dear Reader,

As we reach the conclusion of this book, I want to take a moment to reflect on the journey we've shared. Writing "Project 2025: The Citizen's Guide to America's Next Political Era" has been a labor of love, driven by my deep belief in the power of informed and engaged citizenship.

Throughout these chapters, we've explored the complexities of our political landscape, the transformative potential of Project 2025, and the critical role each of us plays in shaping the future of American democracy.

From understanding governance shifts and navigating political polarization to recognizing the power of civic engagement and the influence of media, we've delved into the heart of what makes our democracy vibrant and resilient.

But this book is just the beginning. The real work begins now, with you and me, and every citizen who cares about the future of our nation. As we look ahead, I want to leave you with a call to action—a reminder that your voice, your vote, and your participation matter.

Get Informed and Stay Engaged

Informed citizens are the cornerstone of a healthy democracy. Make a commitment to stay informed about the issues that matter to you. Seek out reliable sources of information, engage in thoughtful discussions, and question what you read and hear. Knowledge is power, and an informed electorate is essential for holding leaders accountable and making sound decisions.

Vote in Every Election

Voting is one of the most powerful tools we have to influence the direction of our country. Make sure you are registered to vote, and participate in every election, from local school board races to presidential contests. Encourage your friends and family to vote as well. Remember, every vote counts, and collective action can drive significant change.

Engage with Your Community

Community engagement is vital for fostering a sense of belonging and collective responsibility. Attend town hall meetings, join local organizations, and participate in community projects. By working together with your neighbors, you can address local issues and build stronger, more resilient communities.

Advocate for Change

If there are issues you are passionate about, don't be afraid to speak up and advocate for change. Contact your elected officials, support advocacy groups, and use social media to raise awareness. Your voice can make a difference, whether you are fighting for environmental protection, social justice, healthcare reform, or any other cause.

Practice Empathy and Respect

In a polarized political climate, it is more important than ever to practice empathy and respect. Engage in conversations with people who have different perspectives, and listen with an open mind.

Seek common ground and work towards solutions that benefit everyone. Remember, we are all part of the same nation, and our strength lies in our ability to come together despite our differences.

Support Civic Education

Investing in civic education is crucial for the future of our democracy. Support programs that teach the principles of democracy, critical thinking, and media literacy. Encourage young people to get involved in politics and understand the importance of their participation. By fostering a well-informed and engaged next generation, we can ensure the longevity of our democratic institutions.

As we conclude this book, I want to express my heartfelt gratitude for joining me on this journey. Your engagement and curiosity are the keys to unlocking the full potential of Project 2025 and shaping a brighter future for America. Together, we can build a more inclusive, equitable, and resilient democracy.

Remember, the story of America is not just written by its leaders but by each and every one of us. Your voice, your vote, and your actions matter. Let us continue this journey together, striving for a future where democracy thrives and every citizen has the opportunity to flourish.